C0063 93312

KT-157-845

Craft Smart

PAPERCRAFT

Michelle Powell

QED

QED Publishing

QED Project Editor: Ruth Symons

Created for QED Publishing by Tall Tree Ltd
Editor: Catherine Saunders
Designers: Marisa Renzullo and Jonathan Vipond
Illustrator: Barry Croucher
Photography: Michael Wicks

Copyright © QED Publishing 2013

First published in the UK in 2013 by
QED Publishing, a Quarto Group company
6 Blundell Street
London N7 9BH

www.qed-publishing.co.uk

All rights reserved. No part of this publication may be reproduced,
stored in a retrieval system, or transmitted in any form or by any
means, electronic, mechanical, photocopying, recording, or
otherwise, without the prior permission of the publisher, nor be
otherwise circulated in any form of binding or cover other than
that in which it is published and without a similar condition being
imposed on the subsequent purchaser.

A catalogue record for this book is available from the British Library.

ISBN 978 1 78171 098 2

Printed in China

Picture credits

(t=top, b=bottom, l=left, r=right, c=centre, fc=front cover, bc=back cover)
Shutterstock Africa Studio, 3br, lc; Alexandr Makarov, fcr, bctl; Alexandre
Nunes, bct; DenisNata, 8tr; design56, bct, 3, 12c; duniascrap, 3, tr; Elena
Itsenko 3tr, 16r; Elnur, fcc, bct; Feng Yu, fcl, bctr; Getideaka 4tr; Gillian
Mowbray, fcr, bcl; graja, 3br; infografick, 4l; Irina Nartova, fc, bcl, 6, 9, 11, 13,
15, 17, 19, 21, 23, 25, 27, 29, 31; jabiru, 5br; Kitch Bain, fcc, fct; Larina Natalia,
3tc; LittleStocker, 3rc; magicoven, 5b; Malgorzata Kistryn, 3tr; Mighty Sequoia
Studio, 3tc, 4bl; nrt, 3rc; Pamela Uyttendaele, 3b; s1001, 4b; Sirikorn
Techatraibhop, 5rc; Skazka Grez, 4br; SmileStudio, 5tl; spillikin, 3l, 12r;
tsirosn, 3bl; valzan, fcr, bcl; violetblue, 28r; YaiSirichai, 3tr, 4bc.

Note to Adults:

Some children might be able to
do some or all of these projects
on their own, while others might
need more help. These are
projects that you can work on
together, not only to avoid any
problems or accidents, but also
to share in the fun of making crafts.

In preparation of this book, all
due care has been exercised with
regard to the activities and advice
depicted. The publishers regret that
they can accept no liability for any
loss or injury sustained.

At the top of the page for each project you will
find this handy key. It will tell you the difficulty
level to expect from each project:

Quick creative fix

These projects are quick, easy and
perfect for a beginner.

Sharpen your skills

Confident with your beginner skills? Move
onto these slightly tougher projects.

Ready for a challenge

For a challenging project you can really
get stuck into.

Creative masterpiece

Think you can tackle the toughest craft
projects? Have a go at these.

CONTENTS

MATERIALS

origami
paper

Tissue paper
This thin paper is ideal for creating delicate effects, such as flower petals, and for découpage (see page 12).

Crêpe paper
Crêpe paper has been wrinkled up and then flattened, so it is slightly stretchy. It is great for covering objects.

crêpe
paper

Newspaper
Newspaper is great for papier mâché because it is cheap, easy to tear and absorbs the glue well.

Origami paper
You can cut any thin paper into a square for origami. You can also buy square origami paper.

Scrapbooking paper
Patterned papers made for scrapbooking are often thicker than ordinary paper so they are ideal for paper sculptures.

Card
Card is thicker than paper and comes in lots of different weights and colours. Thin card is great for paper crafts, while thicker card is often used as the base for other crafting projects.

Recycled paper
Old paper cups, plates, envelopes, magazines and wrapping paper can all be reused in your craft projects, as well as old cardboard tubes and boxes.

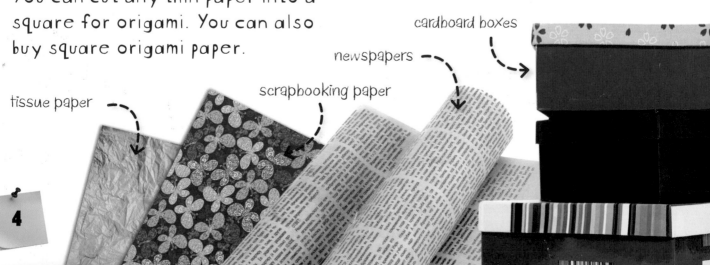

cardboard boxes

newspapers

scrapbooking paper

tissue paper

old cardboard tubes

quilling tool

scoring tool

Glue

All-purpose glue works quickly and sticks different surfaces together well. PVA glue can be watered down and used as varnish.

Glitter glue

This is glitter mixed with glue to make it easy to apply. Make sure you let it dry properly, otherwise it might smudge.

Stick-on gemstones

These sparkly plastic jewels come with glue on the back so they are easy to add to your projects.

Paint

Thick poster paint or acrylic paint is best for adding decoration to your paper crafts.

Tape

Sticky tape is perfect for holding your projects together. Double-sided tape works best when you don't want the tape to show.

Foam pads

Sticky foam pads are similar to double-sided tape, but have a foam layer that creates a three-dimensional effect.

Quilling tool

A quilling tool is a small metal or plastic rod with a slit, fixed into a handle. You thread the end of your paper into the slit and turn the tool to make a coil.

poster paint

Scoring tool

A scoring tool has a metal ball fixed to the end of a handle. It can be used to make an indent in thick paper, which makes folding easier. You can use any pointed, blunt object for scoring, eg a knitting needle, a slim paintbrush handle or a ballpoint pen that has run out of ink.

glitter glue

PVA glue

TECHNIQUES

When folding card or thicker paper it is best to score the paper first, to make folding easier and more even.

SCORING

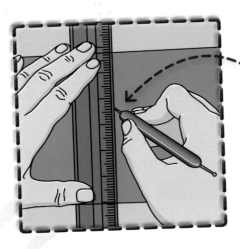

1 Place a ruler where you want to make a fold. Run a scoring tool (see page 5) along the edge of the ruler, pressing down hard to leave a mark. It does not matter which side of the paper you score.

2 The paper or card will fold along the score mark very neatly. Press along the fold with your nail to sharpen it.

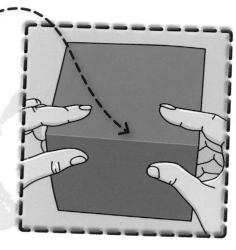

You can also use a scoring tool without a ruler to draw curved lines. This will make a gently curved fold (see page 11).

IRIS FOLDING TEMPLATE

For the iris folding technique on page 18 you will need to trace and use this template. The colours are just for guidance.

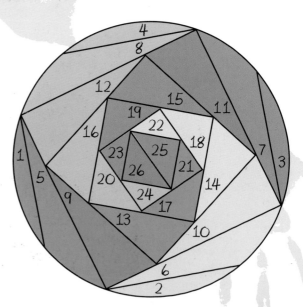

6

PAPIER MÂCHÉ PASTE

Papier mâché uses newspaper and paste. To make your own paste you'll need plain flour, water, PVA glue, salt, a bowl, a whisk, a teaspoon and a small cup.

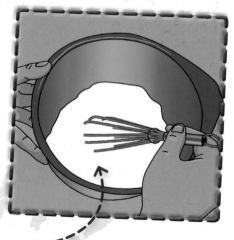

1 Add 1 cup of flour, 1.5 cups of water and 1/3 cup of PVA glue to the bowl. Add a teaspoon of salt to help stop mould from forming.

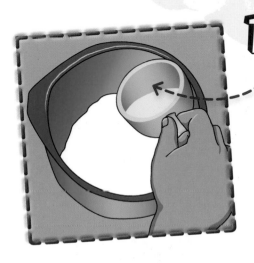

2 Whisk everything in the bowl until the paste is smooth. Add a little more water if you need to. Cover the bowl until you are ready to use it.

CUTTING AN APERTURE

1 Draw a circle on your card. Fold the card in the centre of the circle, but only crease it gently. Use scissors to make a small cut on the fold.

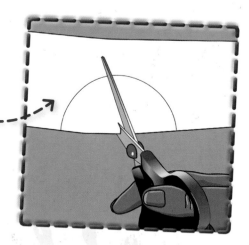

2 Unfold the card. Put the point of the scissors through the hole and cut out the circle.

LOLLIPOP FLOWERS

Unwrap these paper flowers to find a surprise – a delicious lollipop!

YOU WILL NEED:

- Tissue paper
- Crêpe paper
- Thin card
- Lollipop
- Glitter glue
- Sticky tape
- All-purpose glue
- Scissors
- Drinking straw

1 Cut a 9 x 9 cm square of tissue paper. Dab dots of glitter glue onto the outside of the square and allow to dry. Wrap the square around the top of a lolly and secure with tape.

2 Cut three **14 x 14 cm** squares of tissue paper and two **14 x 14 cm** squares of crêpe paper. Fold one square in half diagonally to make a triangle. Fold the triangle in half twice more.

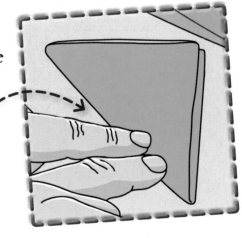

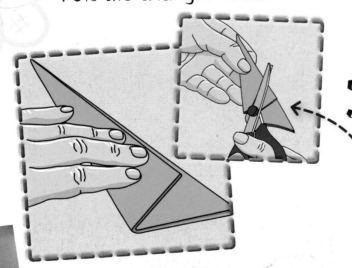

3 Fold in half again to make a narrow triangle. Cut the uneven edge into a curved shape. Cut off the tip of the triangle and then open out to reveal a flower shape. Repeat steps 2 and 3 with all the paper squares.

4 Cut a 9 x 9 cm square of thin card. Follow steps 2 and 3, cutting the tip a little further up to make a larger hole. Reverse every other fold to create a concertina.

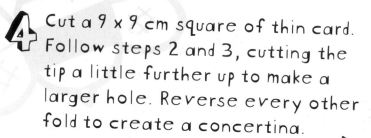

5 Thread all five petal pieces onto the lolly stick, alternating tissue and crêpe paper. Glue the inside of the thin card and stick it to the last petal piece. Add a green straw to make the stem and tape in place.

To make a bee or ladybird, follow step 1 and then cover a small ball of paper with crêpe paper to make a head. Cut card to make wings, and use a pipe cleaner for antennae.

PAPER ROSES

These pretty flowers make a great decoration for any occasion.

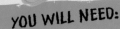

YOU WILL NEED:

- Thin patterned card
- Beads
- All-purpose glue

1 Cut a 14 x 14 cm square of card. Draw a spiral inside the square and then draw a wiggly line along the spiral.

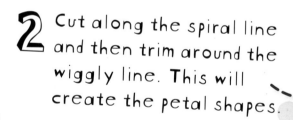

2 Cut along the spiral line and then trim around the wiggly line. This will create the petal shapes.

3 Roll the card up tightly, starting at the centre. Hold the rolled card for a few seconds and then let go, so that it opens out. Glue the end of the strip to the side to hold the shape.

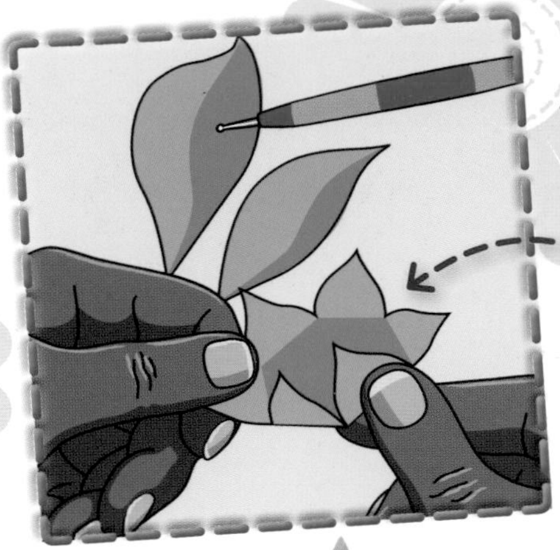

4 Use the template to cut a star shape from green card, then fold up each point of the star. Cut out two leaf shapes. Score and fold to create veins (see page 6).

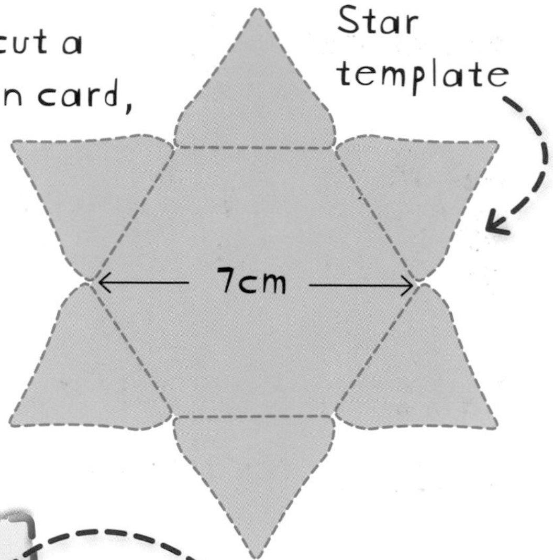

Star template

7cm

5 Glue the coiled flower to the middle of the star. Glue a bead in the centre, then glue the leaves to the back of the star.

You could also make a smaller version to use as a brooch or tiny versions for earrings.

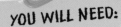

JAM JAR AQUARIUM

Transform an old jam jar into a colourful nightlight with a layered paper and glue technique called découpage.

YOU WILL NEED:

- A clean jam jar with the labels removed
- Tissue paper in various shades and colours, eg blues, greens, purple and orange
- PVA glue
- Glitter glue
- Flat paintbrush
- Scissors
- Battery nightlight

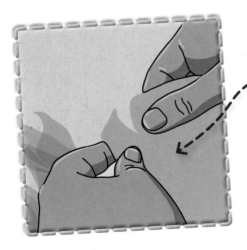

1 Tear your tissue paper into small strips. The strips should be roughly 10 x 2 cm but the size and shape can vary.

2 Paint some glue onto your jar. Add a strip of blue paper and paint more glue on top. Continue adding pale blue and turquoise strips until you have covered the jar.

3 Add some very thin strips of lime green over the blue and some darker blue strips near the bottom.
Leave to dry.

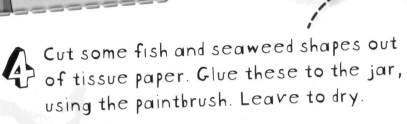

4 Cut some fish and seaweed shapes out of tissue paper. Glue these to the jar, using the paintbrush. Leave to dry.

5 Use glitter glue to add details, such as eyes, fins and bubbles. Leave to dry. Place a battery nightlight inside.

Create your own design. A fairy garden, a sunset or even just a colourful pattern would look fabulous.

FISHY PIÑATA

This traditional Mexican papier mâché toy is filled with sweets and confetti. Take turns to hit it until the sweets fall out!

YOU WILL NEED:

- Newspaper
- Inflated balloon
- Papier mâché paste (see page 7)
- Thick cardboard
- Coloured crêpe paper
- Pin
- Thin, coloured card
- White and green paint
- Paintbrush
- PVA glue
- Scissors
- String

1 Tear a newspaper into squares of about 3 cm. Dip each piece into papier mâché paste and smooth onto the balloon until it is covered. Leave to dry for 4–5 hours. Add three layers, leaving each layer to dry before adding the next.

2 Cut some fins, lips and a tail from thick cardboard. Cover each piece in a layer of papier mâché and leave to dry.

3 Pop the balloon with the pin. Attach the top fin, tail and lips by covering the join with three layers of papier mâché. Let each layer dry before adding the next.

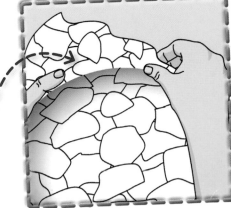

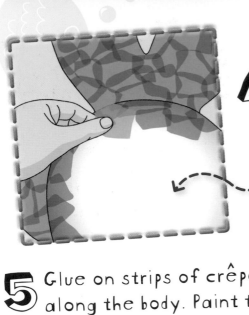

4 Paint the whole fish white and leave to dry. Use watered down PVA glue to apply a layer of crêpe paper over the fins, tail and face of the fish. Leave to dry.

5 Glue on strips of crêpe paper in stripes along the body. Paint the lips. Cut out card circles for the eyes and attach. Glue the side fins into position.

Ask an adult to cut a slit along the side of the top fin. Then fill the piñata with sweets and confetti. Add some string to the top fin and hang the piñata from the ceiling.

MONSTER FOLDING TOY

Make four different monsters with this fun and simple paper toy.

YOU WILL NEED:

- Thin card in two colours
- Paint, pencils or crayons
- All-purpose glue
- Ruler
- Pencil
- Scissors
- Scoring tool (see page 5)

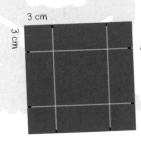

3 cm

3 cm

1 Cut two 12 x 12 cm squares from different colours of thin card. On the back use a pencil to mark eight points, 3 cm away from each corner. Join the opposite points with score lines (see page 6).

2 Turn the two squares over and draw monsters on the fronts. Cut one monster exactly in half horizontally and the other exactly in half vertically.

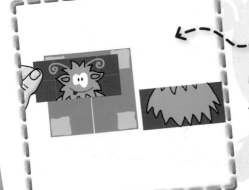

3 Place the two vertically cut pieces face down side by side. Apply glue to the four corners. Stick the two horizontally cut pieces on top, face up, and allow the glue to dry.

4 Fold the top flap up and the bottom one down to reveal a blank side. Decorate this side with another monster. Paint the outer edge of the centre section to match the top and bottom.

5 Fold again, pulling the centre sections out to the sides. You will notice this side is already partially decorated, so just add the rest of the details.

Experiment with your own designs. You could even try using photos for a personalized version.

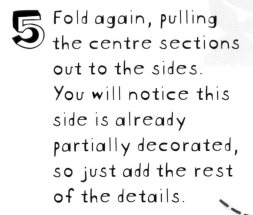

IRIS FOLDED CARD

Make your own greetings cards using a crafting technique called iris folding.

YOU WILL NEED:

- Iris folding template (see page 6)
- 12 × 17.5 cm thin, white card
- 25 × 18 cm thin pink card, folded
- Wrapping paper in four different shades
- Scraps of brown and yellow coloured card
- Glitter glue
- Double-sided sticky tape
- Glue roller or glue stick
- Sticky foam pads
- Sticky tack
- Scissors

1 Cut a 7.5-cm-wide aperture near the top of the white card (see page 7). Use sticky tack to attach the card face down over the template.

7.5 cm

2 Cut four different-coloured strips of paper 2.5 cm wide and 30 cm long. On each strip, fold one long edge over about 5 mm.

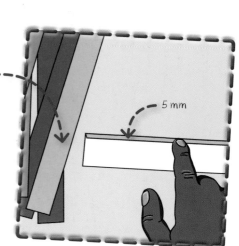

5 mm

3 Take the first strip, face down. Line up the folded edge with section **1** on the template. Cut the strip to fit and glue in place on the edge of the aperture.

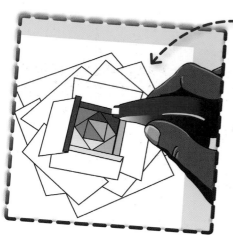

Repeat step 3, adding the strips in order and changing the colour each time. Glue each strip to the back of the previous strips, until you reach the centre.

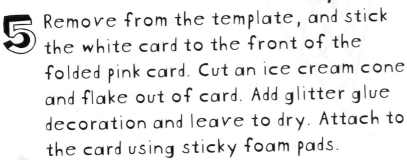

5 Remove from the template, and stick the white card to the front of the folded pink card. Cut an ice cream cone and flake out of card. Add glitter glue decoration and leave to dry. Attach to the card using sticky foam pads.

Create a lovely lollipop card instead. Cut a rectangular lolly stick and attach. Stick a small bag over the front of the circle and tie a bow around it.

ZIG-ZAG PHOTO ALBUM

Cut and fold a single sheet of card to make a fun photo album. It makes a great gift!

YOU WILL NEED:

- 30 × 30 cm thin card
- Scraps of thin card
- Patterned paper
- Ribbon
- Stick-on gemstones
- Glue
- Scissors
- Ruler
- Pencil
- Scoring tool (see page 5)

1 Use a pencil and ruler to mark your square of card at 7.5 cm intervals on all four sides. Join the marks to make a grid of 16 squares.

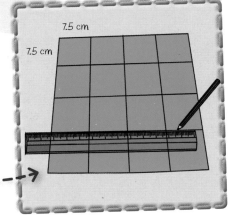

7.5 cm

7.5 cm

2 To create a spiral shape, start at the bottom left corner. Cut three squares to the right, up two squares, left two squares, down one square and then right one square.

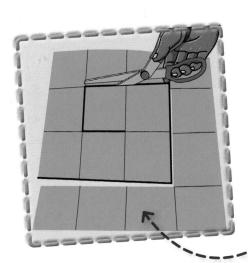

3 Score all the other lines, and fold back and forth on each line to make a concertina-style album.

4 Cut two 40 cm lengths of ribbon and glue them to the first and last pages. Trim your photos to about 6.5 x 5 cm. Cut some strips of patterned paper. Glue the paper strips and photos into the album.

5 Cut some flower shapes from thin card. Glue these to the pages and add stick-on gemstones to decorate. Add a title or message if you like.

Leave your pages plain and add a pretty front and back cover to make a mini notebook or sticker album.

My birthday

ORIGAMI BUTTERFLY

Origami is the Japanese art of paper folding. No glue or scissors are needed!

YOU WILL NEED:

- A 15 x 15 cm square of origami paper (or any patterned paper)

1 With the pattern on the outside, fold the paper in half four ways, from side-to-side and diagonally.

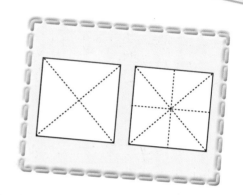

2 Fold the paper in half to make a rectangle. Holding the left side, tuck the right side of the paper towards the centre. Tuck the left side into the centre. You should have a triangle with two flaps on each side.

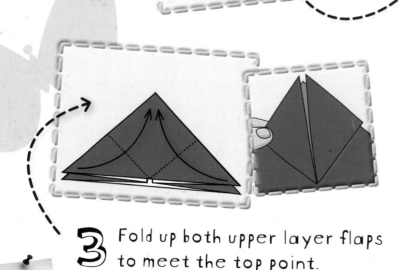

3 Fold up both upper layer flaps to meet the top point.

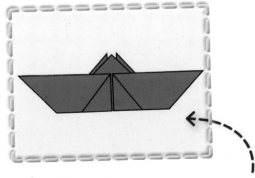

4 Turn it over. Fold all the layers up, leaving a small triangle at the top.

5 Turn it over. Pull the top right flap down gently. The sides will turn up and in. Press them flat. Do the same with the left flap.

6 Turn it over. Fold down the top triangle.

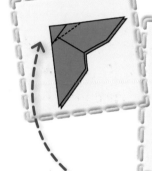

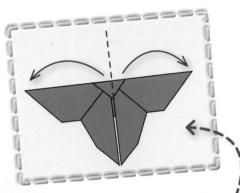

7 Fold in half vertically, folding back so that the wings line up. Keep it folded.

8 Pinch tightly on the small triangle and, while holding, fold back both of the wings. Crease sharply and then allow the wings to fall open.

Make an origami greetings card by attaching your butterfly to a piece of folded card. Add paper clouds and some wire antennae.

KIRIGAMI HANGING STAR

Kirigami is a type of origami that includes paper cutting. Fold, cut and curl to make this star decoration.

YOU WILL NEED:

- Six 10 x 10 cm squares of thick paper or thin card
- String
- Mini stapler or all-purpose glue
- Scissors
- Ruler
- Pencil
- Rubber
- Small hole punch

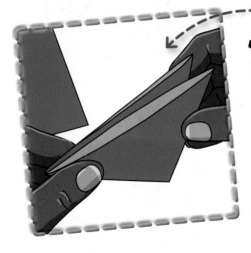

1 Take one square and fold it in half to make a triangle. Then fold it in half again to make a smaller triangle.

2 Draw a line 0.5 cm from the first folded edge. Cut three slits in the other folded edge, stopping when you get to the line. Try to make the cuts just over 1 cm apart and do not cut right across the paper.

3 Rub out the pencil lines and open out the paper. Roll the central two points to the front until they overlap. Staple or glue them together.

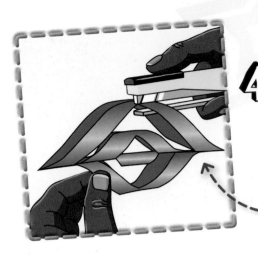

4 Bring the next two points together at the back of the paper and staple. Bring the third set to the front and staple. Staple the last two points at the back. Repeat steps **1** to **4** to make six swirls.

5 Slightly flatten the lower points and staple the swirls together in pairs. Staple two pairs together and then staple or glue the final pair in position. Make a hole in one point and add some string.

Make white stars to look like snowflakes or staple the swirls together to make a chain.

SPANGLY BANGLES

Use papier mâché to create some fun and chunky bangles from newspaper and patterned paper.

YOU WILL NEED:

- Thin card
- Scissors
- Newspaper
- Papier mâché paste (see page 7)
- Patterned paper
- Stick-on gemstones
- White paint
- Sticky tape
- Paintbrush
- Watered-down PVA glue

1 Cut a strip of card 2.5 x 24 cm. Wrap it around the widest part of your hand to form a circle, remembering it will be a little tighter when the papier mâché is applied. Tape the circle. Cut a second strip and tape it on top to make the bangle stronger.

2 Tear a newspaper into long strips about 2 cm wide. Paste your bangle all over and wrap the strips around the whole bangle. Add 2 or 3 layers before leaving it to dry.

3 Add more layers of papier mâché until you have a chunky bangle. Allow it to dry every 3 or 4 layers. Paint with white paint and leave to dry.

4 Tear some strips from the patterned paper. They should be long enough to go around the outside of the bangle and overlap slightly on the inside. Dip the paper strips in the PVA glue, then smooth them onto the bangle.

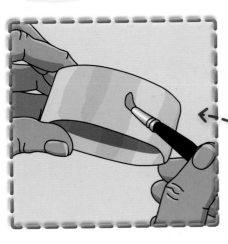

5 Leave the bangle to dry and then add stick-on gemstones. Add another layer of watered-down PVA glue to varnish the bangle. Leave to dry.

Cut thinner strips of card for narrow bangles or cover a cardboard shape in papier mâché to make a matching pendant for a necklace.

QUILLED SHEEP

Use paper strips to create a curly sheep using a technique called quilling. You can roll the strips by hand or use a quilling tool, if you have one.

YOU WILL NEED:

- Black paper strips:
  Legs – 4 strips 1.5 × 30 cm
  Head – 2 strips 0.5 × 30 cm
  Ears – 2 strips 0.5 × 10 cm
- White paper strips:
  Wool and tail –
  9 strips 0.5 × 10 cm
  Body – 1 strip 2 × 30 cm
- White pen
- All-purpose glue
- Sticky tape
- Quilling tool (if you have one)
- Scissors

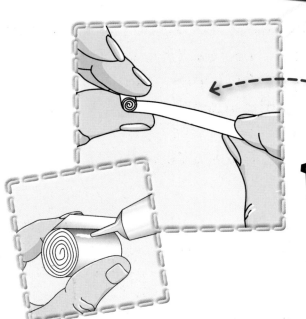

1 Take the white strip for the body and coil it up tightly. It is easier to do this large roll by hand. Allow the coil to unravel until it's about 2.5 cm across. Glue the end in place.

2 Place the end of a 10 cm white strip into the quilling tool and coil it. Remove from the tool. Allow the coil to unravel slightly and glue the end down. Coil all nine pieces and glue eight together in a circle. The last one is the tail.

28

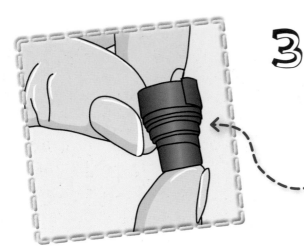

3 Tape the two strips for the head together to make a 60-cm-long strip. Coil it, then allow the roll to unravel slightly and glue the end down. Gently push the centre out to make the head.

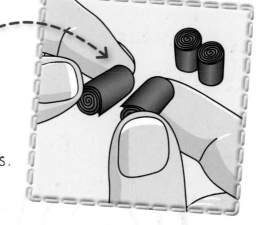

4 Coil a leg strip. Hold the roll tight and put a dot of glue on the end to stick it down. Coil the other three legs. Glue the legs together in pairs.

5 Coil the ears and allow the coils to unravel. Glue the ends and pinch them to make raindrop shapes. Glue the head inside the ring of wool coils and add the ears. Glue the head, wool, legs and tail to the body. Draw on eyes.

Use gold and brown strips to make a lion. Add a brown strip to each leg and another strip to make a longer tail. Add a nose and muzzle and two extra coils for a fuller mane.

PAPER CUP OWL

Transform a paper cup and some paper scraps into a cute owl.

YOU WILL NEED:

- Paper cup
- Thin card in various colours and patterns
- All-purpose glue
- Scoring tool (see page 5)
- Ruler
- Pencil
- Scissors
- Paint
- Paintbrush

1 Paint your cup (if you need to). When it is dry, squash the top part of the cup flat and cut off the rim. Shape the top to create two ears.

2 Cut a rough flower shape out of card. Fold it in half and glue it onto the head to hold the two sides together. Squash the ears into shape.

3 Cut an arched piece of card and fold it in half vertically. Cut three angled slits in the fold and open out. Fold the sides into the centre and cut two angled slits in each fold. Open out and glue onto the cup.

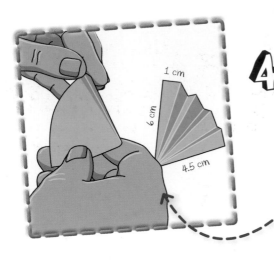

4 Cut two quarter ovals about 6 x 4.5 cm. Mark 1 cm intervals around the curved edge and score lines from the marks to the point. Fold back and forth on each score line to make a concertina. Repeat for the second wing and glue to the sides of the cup.

1 cm

6 cm

4.5 cm

5 To make the eyes, cut out two small, two medium and two large circles. Glue a medium and a small circle on top of each large one, and glue the eyes into position. Cut out a beak and glue in place.

To make a robin, squash the top of the cup. Cut downwards to form a tail, then across the back and up to form the head. Place the eyes and wings on either side of the head.

INDEX